SHE CAME FROM KANSAS

*A Sampler Quilt Celebrating
Remarkable Kansas Women*

By Sandy Humphreys and Sue Horton

SHE CAME FROM KANSAS

A Sampler Quilt Celebrating Remarkable Kansas Women

By Sandy Humphreys and Sue Horton

Editor: Deb Rowden
Designer: Brian Grubb
Photography: Aaron T. Leimkuehler
Illustration: Lon Eric Craven
Technical Editor: Jane Miller, Kathe Dougherty
Photo Editor: Jo Ann Groves

Published by:
Kansas City Star Books
1729 Grand Blvd.
Kansas City, Missouri, USA 64108

First edition, first printing
ISBN: 978-1-61169-098-9

Library of Congress Control Number: 2013941624

Printed in the United States of America by Walsworth Publishing Co., Marceline, MO
To order copies, call StarInfo at (816) 234-4473.

PickleDish.com
The Quilter's Home Page
www.PickleDish.com

KANSAS CITY STAR QUILTS
Continuing the Tradition

SHE CAME FROM KANSAS

Table of Contents

History Lessons   Block

Projects

Location photography throughout the book (such as Mary White's glove, left, and the spectacular rug on page 13) were shot at Red Rocks Historic Site, home of the William Allen White family, in Emporia, Kansas.

About the Authors

SANDY HUMPHREYS

I have always sewed and loved crafts, but I only started quilting in 2000. My friend, Joy, asked me to join a beginner quilt class. She enrolled us in a Thimbleberries Club. As most of you know, that club is not designed for a beginner, nor is it a class. I attended and began quilting. Unfortunately, Joy passed away before getting to attend any meetings. Quilting and the friendships started with quilting helped me through the loss of this lifelong friend and also the passing of my husband, T.G., in 2011.

I enjoy making quilts for my family and friends, teaching quilt classes, and belonging to the Emporia Regional Quilters Guild. My paternal grandmother and an aunt were excellent quilters - I wish I could have shared that experience with them. My daughter, Alicia Redeker; son-in-law, Ryan; and grandsons, Hunter and Dawson have all been recipients of my quilts. Without their support, and that of my husband, I would not have gained the confidence to collaborate on this book with Sue.

SUE HORTON

I have been romanced by quilts my entire life. With two grandmothers, three aunts, a mother, and later a mother-in-law who were all quiltmakers, I believe it was in my DNA! I loved watching them quilt, listening to them talk about quilts, and dreaming of making one myself.

That day finally came in the late 1970s when one of my aunts, Alice Wilson, offered to help me with a log cabin quilt. I remember buying brown calicoes with greens and rust colors, cutting out strips with scissors, and sewing them together - only to find they didn't match up. I was so disappointed and thought, I just don't have it! Aunt Alice calmly took them all from me and returned them several months later sewn up into a beautiful quilt. I was thankful, yet disappointed that I couldn't do what she was able to do. I put my dreams of creating my very own quilt away for a later time in my life.

Then along came the 1980s. One day, I turned on the television and a lady by the name of Eleanor Burns was showing how easy it was to "make a quilt in a day" using something called a rotary cutter. I thought, "Hey, I think I could do that!" I visited with

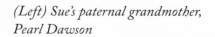

(Left) Sue's paternal grandmother, Pearl Dawson

(Right) Sue's maternal grandmother, Alice Shryock, as a child. Sue remembers later in life, Alice had a needle in hand most evenings, working on her latest quilt.

my mother-in-law, Evelyn, and she encouraged me to give it a try. My very first quilt was a black and white Ohio Star quilt (using a pattern in Eleanor's book of course), a high school graduation present for my son's girlfriend. I was hooked and have been making quilts ever since.

In 2006, I fulfilled another dream with the opening of Prairie Pieces Quilt Shop in Emporia, Kansas.

Today, I still dream of all the quilts I want to make someday. I hope you enjoy this book - perhaps one of these projects will be in your quilting dreams!

Dedication

A special thanks to my husband, Larry, who has encouraged me and is always there with a hug when I need one. One of these days, it will be my turn to do all those dishes, cooking and laundry - I promise. Thank you, Larry!

Acknowledgements

Our heartfelt appreciation and thanks go to the following people. Without them, this book would not have been possible:

Deb Rowden, our editor; Jane Miller, our technical editor; and the staff of Kansas City Star Quilt Books for their assistance and patience in helping us fulfill this dream.

Vickie Vaughn, for helping us write and edit our history lessons, as well as encouraging us.

Myrtle Humphreys, for assisting in our historical research - long distance from Arizona.

Lynne Burns, for having the idea for this Kansas history quilt.

Our sewing group - Jackie G. Davis, Linda Potter, Trish Weidert and Linda Wilson - for their encouragement and willingness to spend long hours making the projects.

Island Batiks, for the fabrics used in Escape to the Tropics.

Jennifer Baldwin at the Red Rocks State Historic Site, William Allen White's home, for arranging photography there.

Bobbie Miller, for naming our quilt She Came from Kansas.

Kathy Smith, Great Plains Quilt Company, Burlingame, for quilting She Came from Kansas.

Linda Wilson, threads!, Emporia, Kansas for quilting Escape to the Tropics.

Barbara Brackman, for the picture of Rose Kretsinger.

A very special thank you to the wonderful quilters who signed up for our block of the month program at Prairie Pieces Quilt Shop. They gave us encouragement, support, and feedback. We both feel we made friendships that will last a lifetime.

Mary White's third floor bedroom at Red Rocks, circa 1921.

6

Introduction

Our *She Came from Kansas* quilt began as an idea from Lynne Burns, a customer and friend. Lynne was doing research on Kansas women for a college paper. It was her idea to design a quilt to honor these women.

We liked the idea, but due to other obligations, it was put on the back burner for a few years. This quilt kept returning to our conversations until finally one day we said, "Are we going to do this or not?" We started by choosing twelve women and picking a quilt block that matched their accomplishment. It was difficult to narrow our choices down to just twelve women. We were amazed at how many women with Kansas connections were the first females in a specific vocation in the nation. We are quilters first but truly enjoyed our historical journey through Kansas.

The quilt was made and became a block of the month project at Prairie Pieces Quilt Shop, Emporia, Ks., in 2012. Each month we met and went over instructions and additional history. It was a well-received program and started many conversations about Kansas history. One month during this meeting, a customer was visiting the shop and wanted to know what was going on. When we explained about our block of the month and the histories, she asked if we ever thought about making it into a book. She introduced herself as Donna di Natale, a Kansas City Star editor. Lo and behold, now we are two Kansas women writing our first quilt book.

Our sampler quilt can be made using almost any fabrics. We used Moda's Kansas Troubles fabrics but you might try 1930s, reproductions, or even batiks like our *Escape to the Tropics* version (page 59). We hope you enjoy making this quilt and the other projects included in our book.

Sandy and Sue

Susan Selby Magoffin
Blazed Trail

7

She Came From Kansas

She Came From Kansas

Machine pieced by Sandy Humphreys.
Machine quilted by Kathy Smith, Burlingame, Kansas.

Finished size: 93" x 93"

Fabric Requirements

Quilt Blocks

1 ⅓ yards total of assorted red prints

1 ⅓ yards total of assorted tan prints

½ yard total of assorted green prints

¼ yard brown print

1 yard total of assorted cream prints

½ yard total of assorted blue prints

½ yard purple

¼ yard rust

¼ yard black

Fat quarter 1 large print (block 11 center)

Fat quarter gold large print (block 6)

Alternate Blocks

1 ½ yards tan

1 ½ yards cream

1 ⅛ yards red

Border

1 yard red

2 ½ yards large print

Binding

¾ yard

Backing

9 yards

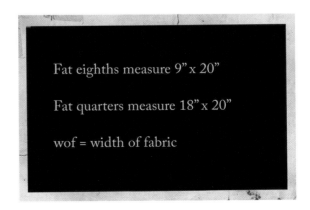

Fat eighths measure 9" x 20"

Fat quarters measure 18" x 20"

wof = width of fabric

BLOCK 1 | Wagon Tracks

Laura Ingalls Wilder

Born: Feb. 7, 1867, Pepin, Wis.

Died: Feb. 10, 1957, Mansfield, Mo.

Photo courtesy of Laura Ingalls Wilder Home Association, Mansfield, Mo.

Laura Ingalls Wilder wrote stories about her family's life on the frontier, which included living in a cabin in southeast Kansas. These stories became the popular "Little House" series of children's books.

The Homestead Act of 1862 made 160 acres available to an eligible person in return for a five-year residency and $18 in filing fees. The opportunity lured the Wilder family to Montgomery County in Kansas, in the fall of 1869. Laura later would write about the cold weather the family experienced that winter. The Wilders' cabin was on the 4.8 million acre Osage Diminished Reserve, which was not open to white settlement. Tensions between the Osage and settlers were strained at that time. In an effort to keep the peace, the government sent soldiers in February 1870, although settlers were not required to move.
The Wilder family decided to leave their cabin in spring 1871 and return to Wisconsin. Wilder would write about an Osage leader who eventually persuaded his people to agree to cede the lands.

The Wilders lived in Wisconsin until 1874, when Laura was seven. They moved near Plum Creek in Walnut Grove, Minn. A couple of years later, the family moved to Iowa, near De Smet in Dakota Territory.

Laura became a schoolteacher in De Smet just before her 16th birthday. She married Almanzo Wilder in 1885. Their daughter, Rose, was born the next year.

Laura Wilder shared her stories about travels to different parts of the frontier with Rose, who had a successful career as an editor. With Laura as author, the women worked together to begin publishing the stories. Her third book, *Little House on the Prairie,* published in 1935, was about the family's experience in Kansas. Laura was too young to remember the details but relied on her family's memories. The setting for the book is about 15 miles southwest of Independence, Kan.

The city has a reconstructed cabin based on her books and a well thought to be hand-dug by her father, Charles Ingalls.

The television series lasted 10 years - from 1974 to 1984 - and brought more fans to her "Little House" books. The series, set in Walnut Grove, Minn., was the story of "Pa and Ma" — Charles and Caroline Ingalls — and Laura, Mary and Carrie.

"…we traveled to the Indian territory … My childish memories told the sound of the war whoop, and I see pictures of painted Indians."

— Laura Ingalls Wilder, February 1918.

Cutting Instructions

Tan: Cut 1 - 3" x wof strip for (A) four-patches.

Green: Cut 2 - 5 ⅞" squares. Cut once on the
        diagonal to make 4 – (B) triangles.

Red: Cut 1 - 3" x wof strip for (A) four-patches.
        Cut 2 - 5 ⅞" squares. Cut once on the
        diagonal to make 4 – (B) triangles.

BLOCK DIAGRAM

Piecing Instructions

1. Sew the tan and red 3" wide strips together.
   Press the seam toward the red strip.

2. Subcut into 10 – 3" wide sections.

   3″   3″

3. Sew together 2 sections to make an
   (A) four-patch. Press the seam
   toward the red.
   Square up to 5 ½". Make 5.

4. Sew a red and green triangle together
   to make a (B) square. Press the seam
   toward the red. Square up to 5 ½".
   Make 4.

5. Refer to the block diagram and stitch the units
   together into 3 rows. Press the seams away from
   the large triangles. Stitch the rows together. The
   unfinished block measures 15 ½" square.

BLOCK 2 | Prohibition

Carrie Nation

Born: Nov. 25, 1846, Garrard County, Ken.

Died: June 9, 1911, Leavenworth, Kan.

Carrie Nation with Bible and hatchet in hand.

The spelling of her first name is ambiguous. Both "Carrie" and "Carry" are considered correct because her father noted the name "Carry" in the family Bible when she was born. Upon beginning her campaign against liquor in the early 20th century, she adopted the name "Carry A. Nation" mainly for its value as a slogan and registered it as a trademark in Kansas.

Carrie was born in Garrard County, Ken., to slave owners George and Mary Campbell Moore. She was in poor health during much of her early life. Her family had several financial setbacks and moved frequently. Many of her family members also suffered from mental illness. Her mother, at times, had delusions of being Queen Victoria. Young Carrie often found refuge in the slave quarters.

During the Civil War, the family moved to Cass County, Mo., but the Union Army ordered them to evacuate. They moved to Kansas City, where Carrie nursed wounded soldiers after raids on Independence, Mo.

In 1865, she met a young physician, Dr. Charles Gloyd, who had fought for Union. By all accounts, he was a severe alcoholic. They married in 1867, but separated soon after the birth of their daughter less than a year later.

After earning her teaching certificate in 1872, she taught school for four years. In 1874, she married David A. Nation, an attorney, minister and newspaper editor. After a failed attempt at farming in Texas, they moved to Medicine Lodge, Kan., where Carrie began her temperance work. She started a branch of the Women's Christian Temperance Union and campaigned for a ban on liquor sales in Kansas. She at first used rocks, then later turned to hatchets to attack bars and saloons.

Cutting Instructions

Brown: Cut 4 - 4 ¼" squares (A).

Green: Cut 8 - 4 ¼" squares (A).
Cut 1 - 2 ⅜" x wof strip for (B)
four-patch blocks.

Tan: Cut 1 - 2 ⅜" x wof strip for (B)
four-patch blocks.

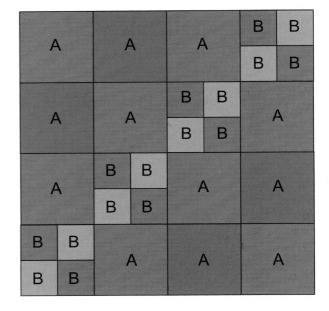

BLOCK DIAGRAM

Piecing Instructions

1. Sew the green and tan 2 ⅜" strips together.
Press the seam towards the green.

2. Subcut into 8 - 2 ⅜" wide sections.

3. Sew together 2 sections to make a
(B) four-patch. Press the seam
toward the green. Square to 4 ¼".
Make 4.

4. Refer to the block diagram and stitch the
units together into 4 rows. Press the seams
of each row in opposite directions. Stitch
the rows together. The unfinished block
measures 15 ½" square.

Hattie McDaniel, 1941

Hattie McDaniel

Born: June 10, 1895, Wichita, Kan.

Died: Oct. 25, 1952, Woodland Hills, Calif.

Hattie McDaniel was the first African-American actress to win an Academy Award. She won the award for Best Supporting Actress for her role as Mammy in "Gone With the Wind."

Born to former slaves, Hattie was the youngest of 13 children. Her father fought in the Civil War and her mother sang religious music. The family moved to Denver in 1900, and Hattie graduated from high school there. Early in life, she worked in her brother's minstrel show and wrote songs as well.

In the 1920s, Hattie started a radio career, singing with the Melody Hounds on a Denver radio station. In 1927, she also recorded many of her songs on the Okeh and Paramount record labels in Chicago.

Then came the 1929 stock market crash. The only work Hattie could find was as a washroom attendant and waitress at Club Madrid in Milwaukee. Despite the owner's reluctance to allow her to perform, she eventually was allowed to take the stage and became a regular performer.

In 1931, Hattie joined family members in Los Angeles. She took jobs as a maid and cook when she could not find film work. When her brother was able to get Hattie a spot on a radio program, she played the title role as a bossy maid who often forgot her place. Her show became a hit, but her salary was so low she had to continue working as a maid.

Her first film appearance was in 1932 in "The Golden West," in which she played a maid. Hattie's film career spans hundreds of films; many of her roles were prominent ones.

She died at age 57 from breast cancer. Because Hollywood Cemetery on Santa Monica Boulevard would not accept black people, she was buried in Rosedale Cemetery.

Cutting Instructions

Cream: Cut 4 – 2" squares (A).

Cut 12 – 2 ⅜" squares for (B) half-square triangles.

Blue: Cut 12 – 2 ⅜" squares for (B) half-square triangles.

Tan: Cut 4 – 6 ½" x 3 ½" rectangles (C).

Red: Cut 1 – 3 ½" square (D).

Green: Cut 4 – 5" squares (E).

Tip:
To make the (B) half-square triangles, you can use your favorite product (such as Thangles or Triangulations). If you use these, skip cutting the 2 ⅜" squares and go to Step 3 after making 24 cream/blue half-square triangles that finish 1 ½".

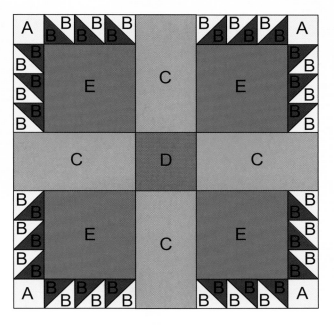

BLOCK DIAGRAM

Piecing Instructions

1. Draw a line diagonally on the wrong side of each cream 2 ⅜" square.

2. Place a 2 ⅜" blue square and a 2 ⅜" cream square with right sides together. Sew ¼" on each side of the diagonal line. Cut on the diagonal line. Press the seam toward the blue triangle. Make 24 – 2" unfinished cream/blue half-square triangles.

3. Stitch together 3 cream/blue half-square triangles. Make 4.

4. Stitch together 3 cream/blue half-square triangles. Add a cream (A) square to the end. Make 4.

5. Stitch a strip of half-square triangles to the side of a green (E) square. Press the seam toward the green square. Now stitch the strip with the cream square to the top of the green square. Press the seam toward the green square. Square up to 6 ½". Make 4.

6. Refer to the block diagram and stitch the units together into 3 rows. Press the seams toward the (C) rectangle. Stitch the rows together. Press the seams toward the middle. The unfinished block measures 15 ½" square.

BLOCK 4 | Lost Propeller

Amelia Earhart

Born: July 24, 1897, Atchison, Kan.

Disappeared: 1937, Pacific Ocean

Ameila Earhart with President Calvin Coolidge, 1928. Photo courtesy of the Library of Congress.

Noted American aviation pioneer and author Amelia Earhart was the first woman to fly solo across the Atlantic Ocean. She set many records, wrote best-selling books and was instrumental in forming the Ninety Nines, an organization of female pilots.

In 1935, Earhart joined the Purdue University aviation department to counsel women on careers and help inspire others with her love of aviation. She was a member of the National Woman's Party and an early supporter of the Equal Rights Amendment. On the day of her marriage to George P. Putnam in 1931, she wrote a letter to him and had it hand-delivered. She wrote, "I want you to understand I shall not hold you to any midaevil [sic] code of faithfulness to me nor shall I consider myself bound to you similarly."

During an attempt to circumnavigate the globe, Earhart and her navigator disappeared over the central Pacific Ocean. Fascination with her life and disappearance continues to this day. A myriad of theories have emerged about her disappearance, but two possibilities have prevailed among researchers and historians. One theory is that her Electra ran out of fuel, and she and Fred Noonan ditched at sea not far from Howland Island. It is the most widely accepted explanation. The second theory is that her flight ended in the Phoenix Islands, 350 miles southeast of Howland. In 1966, CBS Correspondent Fred Goerner published a book claiming Earhart and Noonan were captured and executed by the Japanese on Saipan. Amelia Earhart's birthplace home in Atchison, Kan., is a museum where her artifacts and possessions are on display.

Cutting Instructions

Purple: Cut 1 - 6 ⅞" x wof strip.
Subcut into: 2 - 6 ⅞" squares (A)
4 - 3 ½" squares (B)

Cream: Cut 1 - 6 ⅞" x wof strip.
Subcut into: 2 - 6 ⅞" squares (A)
5 - 3 ½" squares (B)

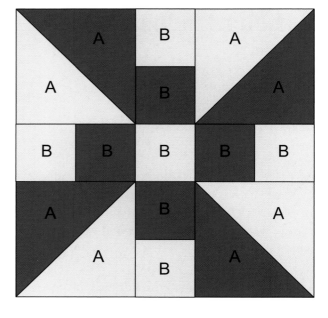

BLOCK DIAGRAM

Piecing Instructions

1. Draw a diagonal line on the back of
each 6 ⅞" cream square.

2. Place a 6 ⅞" purple square and a 6 ⅞" cream
square with right sides together. Sew ¼" on each
side of the diagonal line. Cut on the diagonal
line. Press the seam toward the purple triangle.
Make 4 – 6 ½" unfinished cream/purple half-
square triangles.

3. Stitch together a cream and purple square.
Make 4.

4. Refer to the block diagram and stitch the
units together into 3 rows. Press the seams
toward the (B) squares. Stitch the rows
together. Press the seams toward the
middle. The unfinished block measures
15 ½" square.

22

Photo courtesy of Kansas State Historical Society

Mamie Williams

Born: Dec 12, 1894, Greenwood, S.C.

Died: Dec. 31, 1986, Topeka, Kan.

Mamie graduated at 16 from Topeka High School, one of three African-American girls who graduated that year. Graduating with honors in mathematics and German from Washburn University in 1915, she was the only African-American student that year.

She took an active public role throughout her life. In 1965, she was appointed to the Kansas Commission on the Status of Women. She was a delegate in 1971 to the White House Conference on Aging, and from 1974 to 1976, she was on the Senior Citizens Advisory Council for the Republican Party.

In 1968, Washburn created the AAUW Mamie L. Williams Fellowship Award. The university in 1982 awarded her an honorary doctorate in mathematics.

One of her favorite quotations was "Life is infinitely rich in fine and adequate compensation. Never a door is shut but several windows are opened."

She lived to age 92 and died in a nursing home in Topeka.

Ten years after her death, the Topeka School board named its new science and fine arts magnet school after her.

Mamie Luella Williams was an educator in Topeka for 42 years, including nearly 26 at Buchanan School. She was assistant principal in 1943 at Washington, becoming principal there and later at Monroe before retiring. While she was principal, she also taught and received no extra pay. She retired in 1960.

Mamie and her family moved to Quincy Street in 1900, where she lived the rest of her life. She was the subject of a TV special in 1976, "75 years on Quincy Street."

Cutting Instructions

Tan: Cut 1 - 3 ½" x 2 ½" rectangle (A).
       Cut 1 - 10 ½" x 2 ½" rectangle (C).
       Cut 1 - L (template on page 26).
       Cut 1 - D (template on page 26).

Red: Cut 1 - 2 ½" square (B).
       Cut 1 each (N and M)
       (templates on page 26-27).
       Cut 1 (9 ½" x 2 ½") rectangle (E).
       Cut 1 (3 ½" x 4 ½") rectangle (O).
       Cut 1 (4 ½" x 1 ½") rectangle (Q).
       Cut 1 (1 ½" x 4 ½") rectangle (F).
       Cut 1 (9 ½" x 2 ½") rectangle (G).
       Cut 1 each (6 ½" x 2 ½") rectangles (J and H).
       Cut 1 (2 ½" x 6 ½") rectangle (K).

Cream: Cut 1 (6 ½" x 2 ½") rectangle (I).
       Cut 1 each (2 ½" x 4 ½") rectangles (P and R).

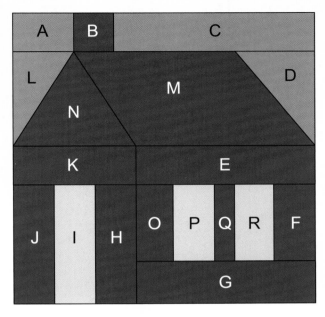

BLOCK DIAGRAM

Piecing Instructions

1. Stitch (A), (B) and (C) together to complete the top row.

   Press seams toward (B).

2. Stitch (L), (N), (M) and (D) together to make the roof row. Press seams toward the red pieces.

3. Stitch (O), (P), (Q), (R) and (F) together. Press seams toward the red. Stitch (E) to the top and (G) to the bottom to complete the windows. Press seams toward (E) and (G).

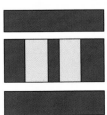

4. Stitch (J), (I) and (H) together. Press seams toward the red. Stitch (K) to the top to complete the door. Press the seam toward (K).

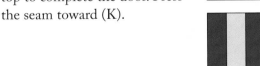

5. Refer to the block diagram and stitch the door to the windows.

6. Follow the block diagram and stitch the 3 rows together. Press seams toward red when possible. The unfinished block measures 15 ½" square.

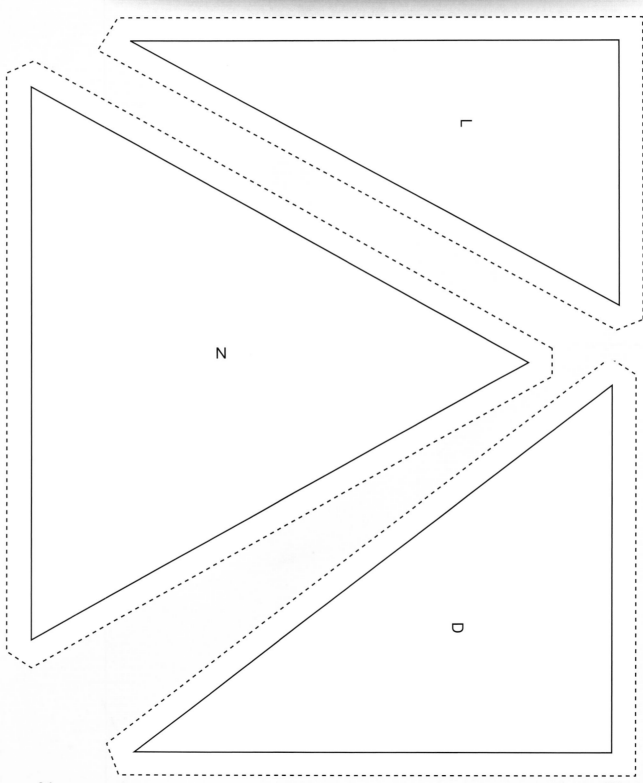

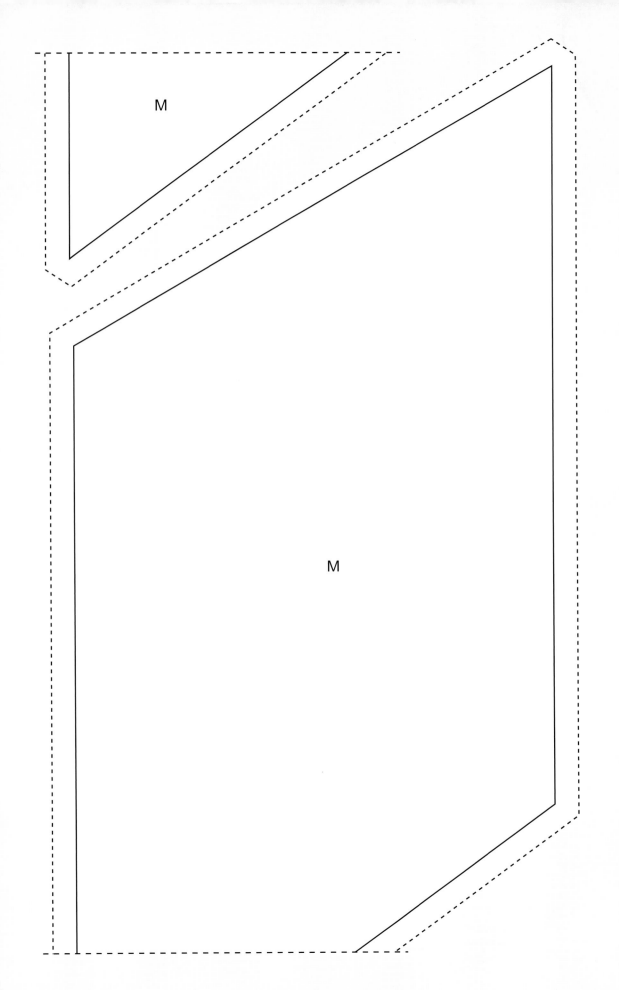

M

M

BLOCK 6 | Lucy's Star

Lucy Hobbs Taylor

Born: 1833, Constable, N.Y.

Died: 1910, Lawrence, Kan.

Photo courtesy of Kansas State Historical Society

Lucy Hobbs Taylor was not only the first female dentist in Kansas, but was very likely the first female dentist in the world.

Orphaned at 12, Lucy became a seamstress to help pay for her schooling. In 1849, she graduated from Franklin Academy in New York. At a time when women were expected to become mothers, nurses or teachers, Lucy sought to be much more. When she was 16, she became a teacher in Michigan and taught for 10 years.

Lucy moved to Cincinnati, where she was denied admission to the Eclectic College of Medicine because of her gender. She finally met Dr. Samuel Wardle, who agreed to let her be his apprentice in his newly established dental office. To support herself, she took in seamstress work. After two years of sewing and her apprenticeship, she met the requirements to apply to the Ohio College of Dental Surgery. Despite her qualifications, she was still denied admission because the college did not accept women.

At 28, with encouragement from Wardle, she opened a dental office in Cincinnati without having a dental degree. She decided to move her practice to Bellevue, Iowa, where she did well. Her reputation grew, and in 1865 she was the first woman to become a member of the Iowa State Dental Society. She attended the American Dental Convention meeting as an Iowa delegate.

Iowa dentists made an appeal at the convention for her to be accepted into a dental college, threatening to boycott schools that would not accept her. The Ohio College of Dental Surgery, which had previously denied her admission, accepted her. She graduated after one session because of her previous practice and experience. In 1866, she became the first woman to receive a doctor of dental surgery degree.

In 1867, she married James M. Taylor, who also became a dentist. They moved to Lawrence, Kan., and established their practice, which focused on women and children. She practiced in Lawrence for more than 40 years, an enormous accomplishment for a woman of that era. When her husband died, she closed their practice and retired from dentistry.

She remained active in civic and political issues, especially the women's suffrage movement.

Since 1983, the American Association of Women Dentists has bestowed the Lucy Hobbs Taylor Award to outstanding women in dentistry. The award is the highest and most prestigious award it presents to its members.

Cutting Instructions

Red: Cut 7 - 3 ⅞" squares for (A) half-square
triangles.

Tan: Cut 2 - 3 ½" squares (B).
Cut 7 - 3 ⅞" squares for (A) half-square
triangles.

Gold large print: Cut 1 - 9 ½" square (C).

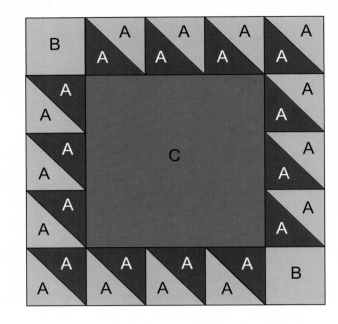

BLOCK DIAGRAM

Piecing Instructions

1. Draw a diagonal line on the back of each
   3 ⅞" tan square.

2. Place a 3 ⅞" red square and a 3 ⅞" tan square
   with right sides together. Sew ¼" on each side
   of the diagonal line. Cut on the diagonal line.
   Press the seam toward the red triangle. Make
   14 – 3 ½" unfinished tan/red (A) half-square
   triangles.

3. Stitch together 3 red/tan (A) half-square
   triangles. Make 2.

4. Stitch to either side of the large print square
   (C). Press seams toward the large square.

5. Stitch together 4 red/tan (A) half-square
   triangles and a tan 3 ½" (B) square. Make 2.

6. Refer to the block diagram and stitch the
   3 rows together. Press the seams toward the
   large square. The unfinished block measures
   15 ½" square.

BLOCK 7 | Courthouse Steps

Susanna Salter

Born: March 21, 1860, Ohio

Died: March 17, 1961, Okla.

When Susanna Madora Kinsey was 12, her family moved to Kansas. At the age of 20, she entered Kansas State Agricultural College (now Kansas State University) as a sophomore. She skipped her freshman year because she completed college level coursework in high school. Six weeks before graduation, she dropped out because of illness.

While she was in college, she met Lewis Salter, an aspiring attorney. He was the son of former Kansas Lt. Gov. Melville Salter.

Susanna and Lewis married soon after and moved to Argonia, Kan., where he managed a hardware store. Her parents soon moved there, bought the store from them and began operating it under the name Kinsey and Salter. Susanna was active in the Woman's Christian Temperance Union and the Prohibition Party, where she met Carrie Nation.

In 1883, she gave birth to the first child born in Argonia. She had eight more children. In 1885, her father was elected the town's first mayor, and her husband was elected city clerk.

On April 4, 1887, when she was 27, she was elected mayor of Argonia. She was the first woman elected mayor in Kansas and to any political office in the United States. The election was just weeks after women gained the right to vote.

She was not informed of her nomination until Election Day. A few of the first voters asked her whether she would run if nominated, and she accepted. Nominated as a joke by 20 men, she later shocked them after receiving two-thirds of the votes. Some of the men who nominated her were on her council, where they grew to respect her. She served for a year and declined to seek re-election.

The town paid her $1 for serving that year, and she spent many times that answering her fan mail. She received many letters from around the world, some from nobility. She died at the age of 101 in Oklahoma and is buried in Argonia, Kansas.

Cutting Instructions

Blue: Cut 2 - 15 ½" x 2 ⅜" rectangles (A).

Brown: Cut 2 - 11 ¾" x 2 ⅜" rectangles (B).

Tan: Cut 2 - 11 ¾" x 2 ⅜" rectangles (B).

Cream: Cut 2 - 8" x 2 ⅜" rectangles (C).

Rust: Cut 2 -8" x 2 ⅜" rectangles (C).

Green: Cut 2 - 4 ¼" x 2 ⅜" rectangles (D).

Red: Cut 1 - 4 ¼" square (E).

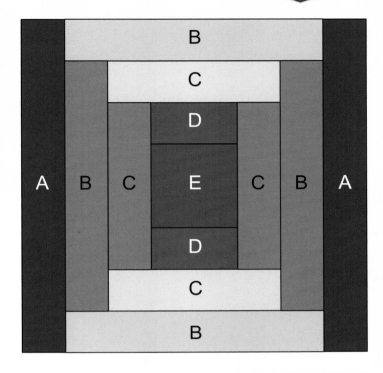

BLOCK DIAGRAM

Piecing Instructions

Note: Refer to the block diagram. Press seams toward the dark fabric.

1. Sew the green (D) 4 ¼" x 2 ⅜" rectangles to the top and bottom of the red 4 ¼" square (E).

2. Sew the rust (C) 8" x 2 ⅜" rectangles to the sides of this center.

3. Sew the cream (C) 8" x 2 ⅜" rectangles to the top and bottom.

4. Sew the brown (B) 11 ¾" x 2 ⅜" rectangles to the sides.

5. Sew the tan (B) 11 ¾" x 2 ⅜" rectangles to the top and bottom.

6. Sew the blue (A) 15 ½" x 2 ⅜" rectangles to each side.

7. The unfinished block measures 15 ½" square.

BLOCK 8 | Rosebud

Rose Kretsinger

Born: 1886, Hope, Kan.

Died: June 23, 1963, St. Frances Hospital,
Wichita, Kan.

Rose Kretsinger, about 1917, courtesy of her family

For the first 12 years of her life, Rose's family lived with her grandparents in Abilene, Kan. Her grandmother taught her to sew. Her family was very oriented to craft making.

In 1899, the family moved to Kansas City. She later attended the School of the Art Institute of Chicago. In 1908, she received a decorative design degree. After spending a year studying in London, Paris, Germany and Switzerland, she returned to Chicago, where she designed jewelry. She was also a fabric designer for Marshall Fields.

After marrying, she moved to Kansas. She had two children, Mary and Bill. Always occupied in creative endeavors, she busied herself upholstering furniture, presenting puppet shows with her children and writing nature poetry.

In 1926, Rose's mother was killed in an automobile accident while returning home from Rose's house in Emporia, Kan. According to Bill Kretsinger, Rose began to quilt after her mother's death. That year, she made her first quilt and found it to be a consoling activity.

Not long afterward, in the early 1930s, the Kansas City Art Museum featured her quilts in a one-woman exhibition.

Along with Carrie A. Hall of Leavenworth, she wrote *Romance of the Patchwork Quilt in America,* a book still available on Ebay, Amazon and other Web sites. Her section is on the art of quilting. The book was the third quilt book of the 20th century.

In 1940, she became a widow.

Her daughter, Mary, donated 12 of Rose's quilts to the Spencer Museum of Art at the University of Kansas in Lawrence. Some of Mary's jewelry is also in the collection.

Two of her patterns, Oriental Poppy and Old Spice, were published in the *Farm Journal.*

Two of her quilts, Paradise Garden and Orchid Wreath, were selected in 1999 for the 20th Century's 100 Best American Quilts at the International Quilt Festival in Houston.

Cutting Instructions

Green: Cut 4 - 3 ⅜" squares for (A) half-square
triangles.

Cream: Cut 4 - 3 ⅜" squares for (A) half-square
triangles.
Cut 2 - 3 ⅜" squares. Cut once on the
diagonal to make 4 - (A) triangles.
Cut 2 - 8 ⅜" squares. Cut once on the
diagonal to make 4 - (B) triangles.

Purple: Cut 2 - 5 ⅞" squares. Cut once on the
diagonal to make 4 - (C) triangles.

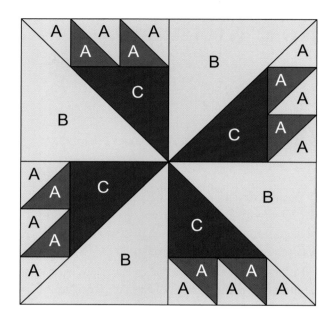

BLOCK DIAGRAM

Piecing Instructions

1. Draw a line diagonally on the wrong
side of each cream 3 ⅜" square.

2. Place a 3 ⅜" green square and a 3 ⅜" cream
square with right sides together. Sew ¼" on each
side of the diagonal line. Cut on the diagonal
line. Press the seam toward the green triangle.
Make 8 – 3" unfinished cream/green half-square
triangles.

3. Stitch 2 half-square triangles together. Stitch an
(A) triangle to the left side. Make 4.

4. Sew the purple triangle (C) to the bottom of
the half-square triangle unit. Make 4.

5. Sew a cream (B) triangle to this
unit to complete the unit. Make 4.

6. Refer to the block diagram and stitch the units
into 2 rows. Press the seam toward the (B)
triangle. Stitch the rows together. The
unfinished block measures 15 ½" square.

BLOCK 9 | Road to the White House

Kathryn O'Loughlin McCarthy

Born: April 24, 1894, near Hays, Kan.

Died: Jan. 16, 1952, Hays, Kan.

Photo courtesy of Kansas State Historical Society

A native of Hays, Kan., Kathryn Ellen O'Loughlin was born at a time when Kansas wheat farmers were protesting corporate interest in their crop, especially the railroads and the commodities market. Kathryn grew up to support New Deal legislation in Congress, particularly the Agricultural Adjustment Act, which offered farmers a way to deal with crop surpluses.

She graduated in 1917 from the State Teachers College in Hays, then headed to the prestigious University of Chicago Law School. After graduating in 1920, she returned to Kansas and in 1921 was chosen clerk of the Judiciary Committee of the Kansas House of Representatives. In traditionally Republican Kansas, she was at a disadvantage as a Democrat. However, by 1930 the state's economy was plummeting and she won election to the state legislature. After only one term there, she ran for Congress in 1932 and won, having been swept along by the tide of the New Deal, a series of programs initiated by presidential candidate Franklin D. Roosevelt that focused on what historians call the "3Rs": relief, recovery and reform.

Democratic congressional leaders failed to give her the committee assignments that were most relevant to her constituents. She protested and won a transfer from Insular Affairs to Education, where she worked for increased vocational funding. She also supported the Agricultural Adjustment Act, by paying farmers subsidies not to plant part of their land. Its purpose was to reduce crop surplus, and a tax on companies that processed farm products paid for the subsidies. That same law proved to be a factor in her loss in the next election, however, as farmers found the bureaucratic process of applying for subsidies too frustrating and did not vote for her again.

She returned with her new husband, Kansas State Sen. Daniel McCarthy, to Hays, where they both practiced law. She also opened a car dealership.

During her lifetime, Kathryn O'Loughlin McCarthy remained a humanitarian, serving with many philanthropic organizations. She promoted the racial integration of Fort Hays State University by paying the tuition of many black students and inviting them to live in her home. She also paid the way for many deserving high school students to attend St. Joseph's Military Academy and St. Francis Seminary. O'Loughlin Elementary School in Hays bears her name in tribute to her caring spirit.

Cutting Instructions

Cream: Cut 2 - 5 ½" squares (A).
        Cut 2 - 3" squares (C).

Black: Cut 6 - 3" squares (C).
        Cut 2 - 5 ⅞" squares for (B) half-square
        triangles.

Red: Cut 2 - 5 ⅞" squares for (B) half-square
        triangles.
        Cut 4 - 3" squares (C).

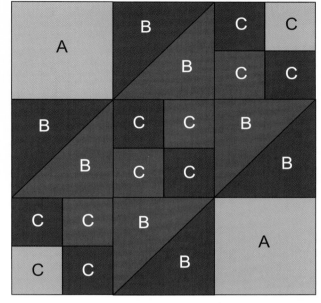

BLOCK DIAGRAM

Piecing Instructions

1. Draw a line diagonally on the wrong
   side of each red 5 ⅞" square.

2. Place a 5 ⅞" black square and a 5 ⅞" red square
   with right sides together. Sew ¼" on each side
   of the diagonal line. Cut on the diagonal line.
   Press the seam toward the black triangle. Make
   4 – 5 ½" unfinished red/black squares.

3. Stitch together 2 black (C) squares, 1 cream (C)
   square and 1 red (C) square to make a four-
   patch unit. Press the seam toward the black
   when possible. Square to 5 ½"
   unfinished. Make 2.

4. Stitch together 2 black (C) squares and 2 red
   (C) squares. Press the seam toward
   the black when possible. Square to
   5 ½" unfinished.

5. Refer to the block diagram and stitch the units
   together into 3 rows. Press the seams away from
   the triangles. Stitch the rows together. The
   unfinished block measures 15 ½" square.

BLOCK 10 | Red Cross

Courtesy Library of Congress Prints and Photographs Division

Mary Ann Bickerdyke

Born: July 19, 1817, Knox County, Ohio

Died: Nov. 8, 1901, Bunker Hill, Kan.

Mother Bickerdyke became the best known, most colorful and probably most resourceful Civil War nurse. Widowed two years before the war began, she supported herself and her two sons by practicing as a "botanic physician" in Galesburg, Ill.

During the Civil War, a young Union volunteer physician wrote home about the filthy military hospitals in Cairo, Ill. Residents collected $500 in supplies and asked Bickerdyke to deliver them. After going to Cairo, she stayed there as an unofficial nurse. She organized the hospitals and gained General Ulysses S. Grant's appreciation. Grant sanctioned her efforts, and when his army moved down the Mississippi, Mother Bickerdyke went too, setting up hospitals. Sherman was especially fond of this volunteer nurse, and supposedly she was the only woman he would allow in his camp.

By the end of the war, with the help of the U.S. Sanitary Commission, Mother Bickerdyke had built 300 hospitals and aided the wounded on 19 battlefields, including the Battle of Shiloh and Sherman's March to the Sea. Bickerdyke was so loved by the Army that soldiers would cheer her as they would a general when she appeared. At Sherman's request, she rode at the head of the XV Corps in the Grand Review in Washington at the end of the war.

When the war ended, she worked for the Salvation Army in San Francisco. She also became an attorney, helping former Union soldiers with legal issues. She then ran a hotel in Salina, Kan. In 1886, she received a special pension of $25 a month from Congress and retired to Bunker Hill, Kan.

Cutting Instructions

Cream: Cut 2 - 3 ⅞" squares for (A) half-square triangles.

Cut 6 – 3 ⅞" squares. Cut once on the diagonal to make 12 (A) triangles.

Cut 4 - 3 ½" squares (B).

Red: Cut 5 - 3 ½" squares (B).

Black: Cut 2 - 3 ⅞" squares for (A) half-square triangles.

Cut 4 template (C).

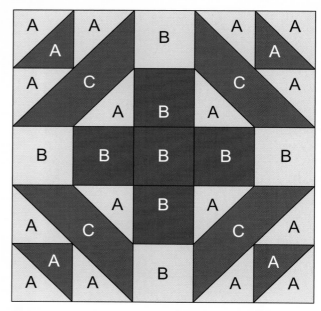

BLOCK DIAGRAM

Piecing Instructions

1. Draw a line diagonally on the wrong side of both cream 3 ⅞" squares.

2. Place a 3 ⅞" black square and a 3 ⅞" cream square with right sides together. Sew ¼" on each side of the diagonal line. Cut on the diagonal line. Press the seam toward the black triangle. Make 4 – 3 ½" unfinished cream/black half-square triangles.

3. Sew an (A) triangle to the right side and the bottom of each (A) half-square triangle unit. Make 4.

4. Add the (C) piece. Make 4.

5. Add an (A) triangle to complete the unit. Square to 6 1⁄2". Make 4.

6. Sew a cream (B) square and a red (B) square together. Press the seam toward the red. Make 4.

7. Refer to the block diagram and stitch the units into 3 rows. Press the seam toward the squares where possible. Stitch the rows together. The unfinished block measures 15 ½" square.

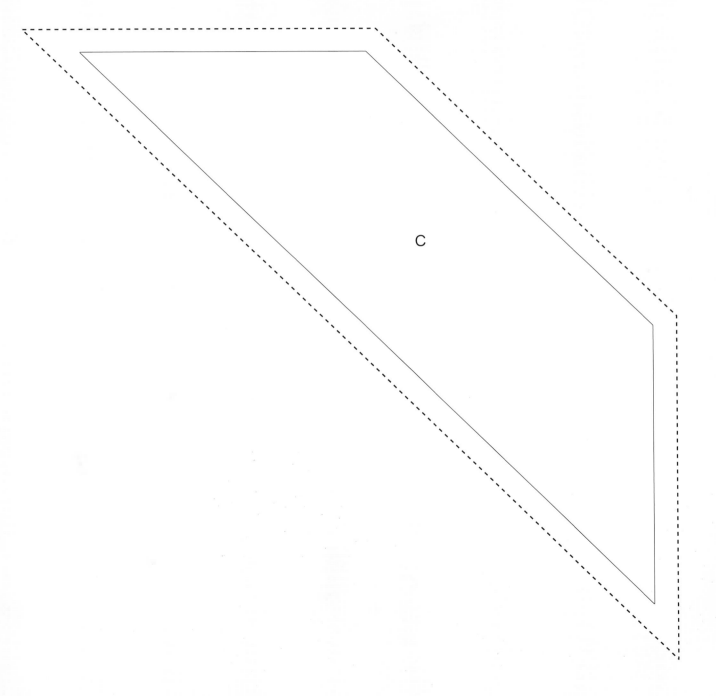

C

BLOCK 11 | Kiowa Star

Mabel Chase

Born: April 15, 1876, Charlottesville, Ind.

Died: 1962, Pea Ridge, Ark.

Photo courtesy of Kansas State Historical Society.

Mabel Brown came to Kansas with her family in 1896. A few years later, she married Frank Chase, who had a veterinary hospital. They had two sons and two daughters.

In 1923, Frank became the sheriff of Kiowa County. He appointed Mabel an undersheriff, and she also did paperwork for him.

In Kansas at that time, sheriffs could serve only two consecutive terms. She was encouraged to run because it was thought she would appoint her husband undersheriff. It was not an easy race because party-line democrats had a candidate who ran against her in the primary. She won the primary by 75 votes and the general election by 118 votes.

In 1927, Mabel was sworn in as sheriff, becoming the first woman elected to that position in the United States. The first female sheriff in the U.S. was Texan Emma Bannister in 1918, appointed after her husband died.

Mabel served one term, 1926 to 1928. During that time, Frank convinced the County Commission to purchase a machine gun and have their 1926 Hudson armor plated and have bulletproof glass put in it. It was not known whether Mabel ever used the machine gun.

She received letters of congratulations and newspaper coverage across the country and in England. In her first year of office, she led a raid on bootleggers. Police confiscated a still and 52 gallons of mash.

Mabel and Frank ended their careers when her term expired. They retired to Arkansas, where she died in 1962.

Cutting Instructions

Blue: Cut 2 – template (A).
      Cut 2 – template (B).
      Cut 2 - template (C).

Large print: Cut 1 - template (E).

Gold: Cut 6 - template (D).

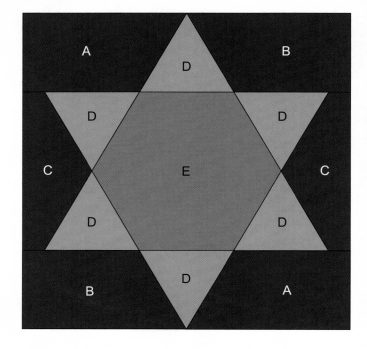

Piecing Instructions

1. Sew 1 (D) to the bottom of template (E). Add a (D) to each side at the top.

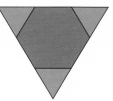

2. Sew (C) and (D) together. Add (B) to the bottom. Refer to the block diagram and stitch to the left side of (E).

3. Repeat for the other side. Sew (C) and (D) together. Add (A) to the bottom. Refer to the block diagram and stitch to the right side of (E).

4. Stitch together (A), (D) and (B) to make the top row.

5. Refer to the block diagram and stitch the 2 rows together. The unfinished block measures 15 ½" square.

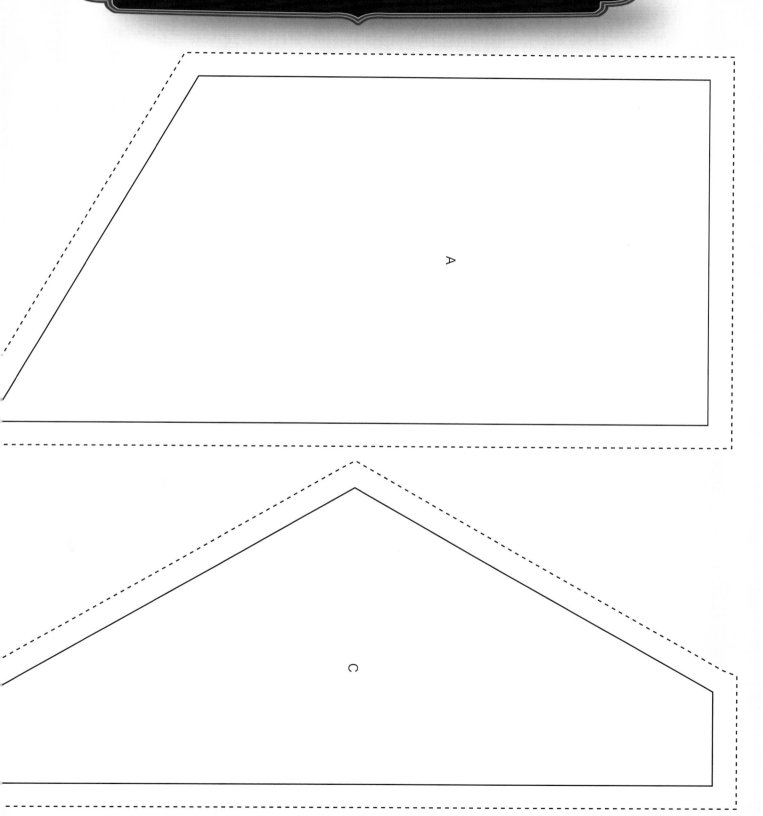

A

C

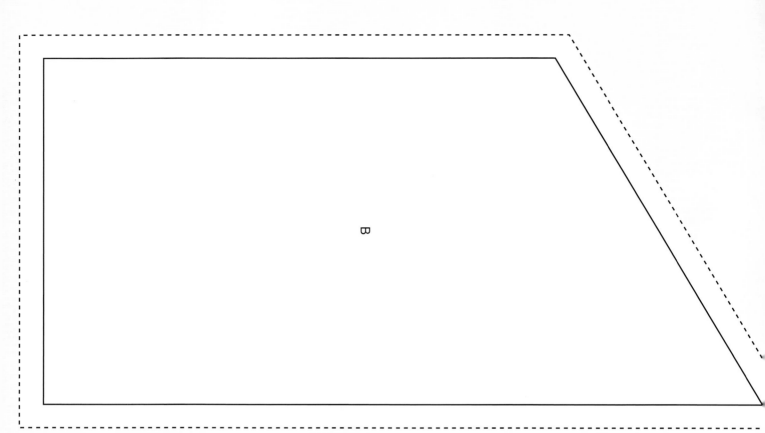

B

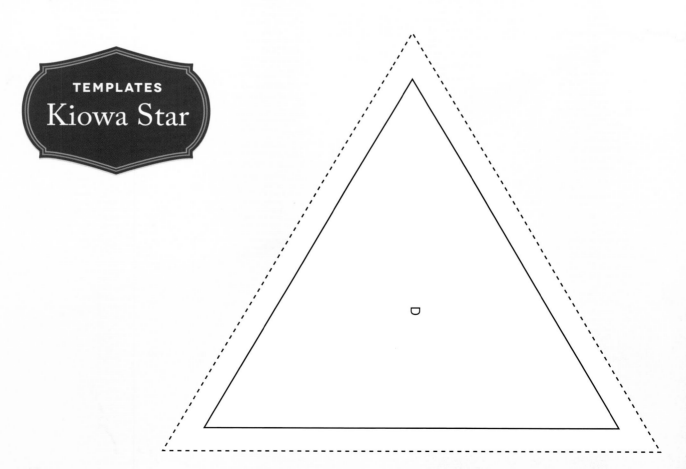

TEMPLATES
Kiowa Star

D

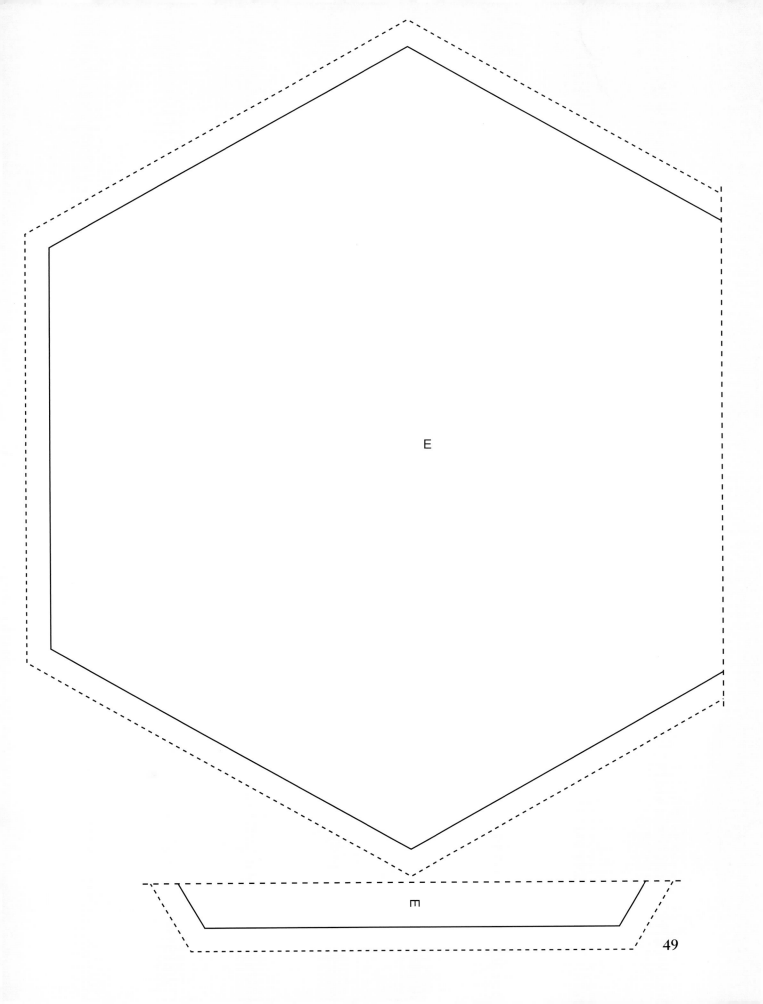

E

m

BLOCK 12 | Blazed Trail

Susan Magoffin

Born: July 30, 1827, near Danville, Ken.

Died: Oct. 26, 1855, St. Louis, Mo.

Born to a wealthy family in Kentucky, Susan Shelby had a sheltered upbringing. She married Samuel Magoffin on Nov. 25, 1845. Even though he, too, was from a wealthy family, Samuel had known the frontier because he and his brother were involved with the Santa Fe trade.

Susan was the first woman to travel on the Santa Fe Trail. While traveling, she kept a journal of her experiences. Because of their wealth, she rode in her own carriage and rested in a tent with servants and Ring, her dog.

After leaving Independence, Mo., they traveled "down the Santa Fe Trail and into Mexico," a phrase she would later use when her journal was published. They traveled through what is now Kansas, Colorado and New Mexico. She kept her journal to share with her family back home.

The first part of her journal tells of the people, animals and plants she came upon in Kansas prairies. She described buffalo as "very ugly, ill-shapen things with their long shaggy hair over their heads and the great hump on their backs." She stopped to gather flowers along the way, sometimes asking her Mexican servants to get them for her.

As they traveled through Kansas near Ash Creek and Pawnee Rock, her carriage upset and she suffered a miscarriage. There is a historic marker, No. 52, near their crossing. It is three miles southwest of Pawnee Rock, considered to be the halfway point along the Santa Fe Trail.

When they reached Mexico, she contracted yellow fever. The rest of their journey was plagued with sickness.

Once back home in St. Louis, she gave birth to two daughters. Shortly after her second daughter was born in 1855, she died.

Her journal is an important part of America's history of the Santa Fe Trail. Its descriptions of the sights and people she encountered allow for a woman's perspective of the journey. Her journal also addresses the Mexican-American War and the trials and tribulations of the traders who traveled the Santa Fe Trail.

Cutting Instructions

Tan: Cut 10 - 2 ⅜" squares (A).
Cut 4 - 4 ¼" x 2 ⅜" rectangles (B).
Cut 4 - 2 ¾" squares for (C) half-square triangles.
Cut 4 - 4 ¼" squares (D).

Rust: Cut 6 - 2 ⅜" squares (A).
Cut 8 - 4 ¼" x 2 ⅜" rectangles (B).
Cut 4 - 2 ¾" squares for (C) half-square triangles.

BLOCK DIAGRAM

Piecing Instructions

1. Draw a line diagonally on the wrong side of each tan 2 ¾" square.

2. Place a 2 ¾" rust square and a 2 ¾" tan square with right sides together. Sew ¼" on each side of the diagonal line. Cut on the diagonal line. Press the seam toward the rust triangle. Make 8 – 2 ⅜" unfinished tan/rust half-square triangles.

3. Stitch together 2 (C) half-square triangles. Make 2.

4. Stitch together another set of 2 (C) half-square triangles. Make 2.

5. Refer to the block diagram and lay out the units into 6 rows. Note the orientation of the (C) half-square triangles. Stitch the units into rows, pressing the seams in opposite directions. Stitch the rows together. The unfinished block measures 15 ½" square.

Finishing Your Quilt

Here are instructions for making the alternate blocks and pieced border to finish your sampler quilt.

Alternate Block

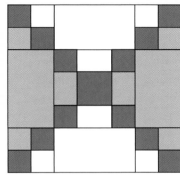

Make 13.

Cutting Instructions

Red: Cut 12 - 2 ½" x wof strips.
         Cut 2 - 3 ½" x wof strips.

Tan: Cut 8 - 2 ½" x wof strips.
         Cut 6 - 4 ½" x wof strips.
         Subcut into: 26 - 7 ½" x 4 ½" rectangles.

Cream: Cut 4 - 2 ½" x wof strips.
         Cut 2 - 3 ½" x wof strips.
         Cut 6 - 4 ½"x wof strips.
         Subcut into: 26 -7 ½" x 4 ½" rectangles.

Piecing Instructions

1. Sew a tan and red 2 ½" strip together. Press the seam toward the red strip. Make 4. Subcut into 52 – 2 ½" segments.

2½"

2. Sew a cream and red 2 ½" strip together. Press the seam toward the red strip. Make 4. Subcut into 52 – 2 ½" segments.

2½"

3. Join a tan/red segment with a cream/red segment to make 52 four-patch units. These are for the 4 corners.

4. Sew a red 2 ½" strip on each side of a cream 3 ½" strip. Press the seam toward the red strips. Make 2. Subcut into 26 – 2 ½" segments.

2½"

5. Sew a tan 2 ½" strip on each side of a red 3 ½" strip. Press the seam toward the red strip. Make 2. Subcut into 13 – 3 ½" wide segments.

3½"

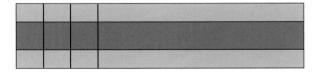

6. Stitch a red/cream/red segment to the top and bottom of a tan/red/tan segment to make the center nine-patch. Press the seams toward the center. Make 13.

7. Refer to the block diagram and stitch the units into 3 rows, adding the tan and cream rectangles. Press the seams toward the rectangles. Stitch the rows together. Make 13. The unfinished block measures 15 ½" square.

Pieced Border

Cutting Instructions

Red: Cut 4 – 2 ½" x wof strips.
Cut 2 – 3 ½" x wof strips.
Cut 6 – 1 ½" x wof strips.

Print: Cut 3 – 2 ½" x wof strips.
Cut 2 – 3 ½" x wof strips.
Cut 5 – 4 ½" x wof strips.
Subcut into: 20 – 5 ½" x 4 ½" (A) rectangles,
and 8 – 7 ½" x 4 ½" (E) rectangles.
Cut 6 – 8 ½" x wof strips.

Pieced Border Blocks

1. Sew a print and red 2 ½" strip together. Press the seam toward the red strip. Make 2. Subcut into 40 – 2 ½" segments.

2½"

2. Join 2 print/red segments to make 20 four-patch units. Set these (D) four-patches aside.

3. Sew a print 2 ½" strip and a red 3 ½" strip together. Press the seam toward the red strip. Make 2. Subcut into 12 – 3 ½" wide segments. Set these (B/C) center units aside.

3½"

4. Sew a print 3 ½" strip and a red 2 ½" strip together. Press the seam toward the red strip. Make 2. Subcut into 20 – 2 ½" wide segments. Set these (B/D) side units aside.

2½"

Assemble Pieced Border Block

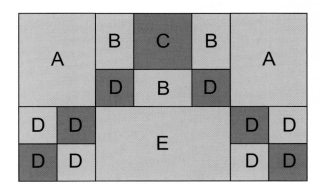

Piecing Instructions

1. Stitch a (B/D) side unit and a (B/C) center unit together. Press the seams toward the center. Make 8.

2. Stitch a (A) print 4 ½" x 5 ½" rectangle to each side. Press the seams toward the rectangles. Make 8.

3. Stitch a (D) four-patch to each side of a (E) print 4 ½" x 7 ½" rectangle. Press the seams toward the rectangles. Make 8.

4. Refer to the block diagram and stitch the rows together. Make 8. The unfinished block measures 9 ½" x 15 ½".

Assemble Pieced Border Corner Block

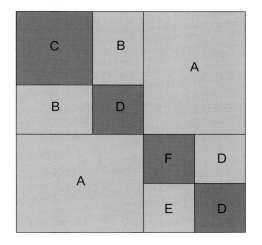

Piecing Instructions

1. Stitch a (B/D) side unit and a (B/C) center unit together. Press the seams toward the center unit. Make 4.

2. Stitch a print 4 ½" x 5 ½" A rectangle to the right side. Press the seam toward the rectangle. Make 4.

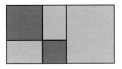

3. Stitch a print 4 ½" x 5 ½" A rectangle to the left side of a four-patch. Press the seam toward the rectangle. Make 4.

4. Refer to the block diagram and stitch the rows together. Make 4. The unfinished block measures 9 ½" square.

Assemble Pieced Border Alternate Block

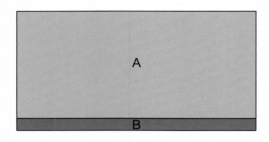

Piecing Instructions

1. Sew a print 8 ½" strip and red 1 ½" strip together. Press the seam toward the red strip. Make 6. Subcut into 12 – 15 ½" segments.

2. The unfinished block measures 9 ½" x 15 ½".

Quilt Assembly

1. Lay out the 12 blocks, 13 alternate blocks, 8 pieced border blocks, 12 pieced border alternate blocks and 4 pieced border corner blocks as shown in the Assembly Diagram.

2. Join the blocks into rows. Stitch the rows together to complete the quilt top.

Finishing

1. Divide the backing into 3 - 3 yard lengths. Join them lengthwise.

2. Layer the backing, batting and quilt top; baste.

3. Quilt as desired. Our quilt was quilted in an allover design to allow the blocks to stand out. Escape to the Tropics was custom quilted.

4. Join (11) 2 1/4" wide binding strips into 1 continuous piece for straight-grain binding. Add binding to quilt.

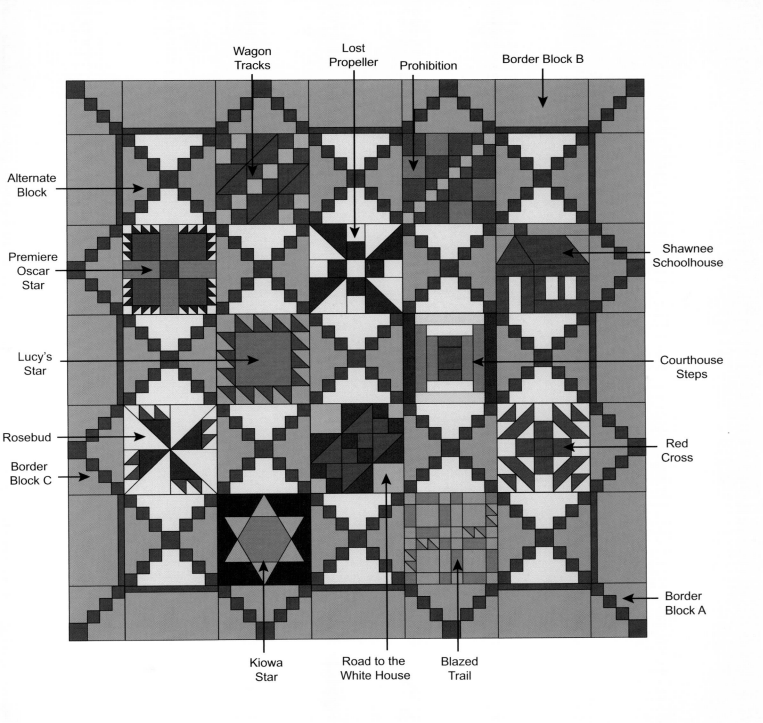

Wagon Tracks

Lost Propeller

Prohibition

Border Block B

Alternate Block

Premiere Oscar Star

Shawnee Schoolhouse

Lucy's Star

Courthouse Steps

Rosebud

Border Block C

Red Cross

Border Block A

Kiowa Star

Road to the White House

Blazed Trail

ASSEMBLY DIAGRAM

Rose Kretsinger
Rosebud

We embroidered the names of the women and the name of the block representing
them in the alternate block. You could do this by hand or machine –
or even pigma pen.

Escape to the Tropics

Made by Jackie Davis, quilted by Linda Wilson | 93" X 93"

Jackie used a completely different palette than the original She Came from Kansas *quilt.*
We all had a hard time waiting for it to come together so we could stand back and say "wow!"
You can almost feel the island breeze from the swaying palm trees quilted on this quilt!

THE EMPORIA GAZETTE

Lucy's Choice Table Runner

21 ½" X 51 ½"

Made and quilted by Trish Weidert

Trish has always liked the Sawtooth block so it wasn't hard for her to take this block and create this table runner. Trish designed, pieced, and quilted this project using Moda's Kansas Troubles fabric.

Fabric Requirements

Red: ⅓ yard

Purple: ⅓ yard

Green: ⅓ yard

Background and binding: 1 yard

Batting: 2 yards (we like thin Thermore polyester)

Backing: 1 ½ yards

Note: We used one fabric of each color for the center piece and 4 different fabrics of each color for the half-square triangles.

Cutting Instructions for 1 Block

Print (red, purple or green) for center square:
Cut 1 - 9 ½" square (C).

Background: Cut 2 - 3 ½" squares (B).

Cut 7 - 3 ⅞" squares for (A) half-square triangles.

Color matching center square print:
Cut 7 - 3 ⅞" squares for (A) half-square triangles.

Block Assembly

Follow the Lucy's Star block instructions on page 30 and make 1 block of each color. Press the seams open. Sew the 3 blocks together as shown in the photo. You may arrange them to make flying geese or turn them a different way to make another pattern.

Borders

Cutting Instructions

Background: Cut 22 - 3 ⅞" squares.
Red, purple and green:
For each color, cut 8 - 3 ⅞" squares (2 are extra).
Make 44 half-square triangles.

Assembly Instructions

Sew 15 half-square triangles together to make each side border and attach. Sew 7 half-square triangles together to make the top and bottom borders and attach. Press.

Finishing

Layer the backing, batting, and top. Pin or baste them together and quilt as desired.

Cut 4 – 2 ¼" strips of the background fabric for the binding. Sew the strips together using diagonal seams. Trim the seams and press open. Fold the binding in half lengthwise and press. Attach to your table runner top using mitered corners. Fold over to the back and finish by hand.

Born in Kansas Doll Quilt/Wallhanging

20" X 25" | *Made and quilted by Linda Wilson*

Linda took some blocks from the original She Came from Kansas *quilt and downsized them using paper-piecing methods. This quilt would be a great wallhanging or doll quilt.*

Fabric Requirements

Various scraps or fat quarters for paper piecing, alternate blocks and Prairie Points. If using fat quarters, you'll need at least 2 lights, 2 mediums and 2 darks for variety.

¼ yard green print for sashing and binding

⅓ yard tan print for outer border

32 – ¼" buttons (optional)

Cutting Instructions

When cutting the patches for paper piecing, make sure the fabric patch covers the entire area and the edges extend well past the sewing lines.

Various fabrics: Cut 6 – 4 ½" squares for alternate blocks.
Cut 32 – 3" squares for Prairie Points.

Green print: Cut 8 – 1 ½" x 4 ½" strips for vertical sashing.
Cut 5 – 1 ½" x 14 ½" strips for horizontal sashing.
Cut 2 – 1 ½" x 21 ½" strips for narrow side border.
Cut 3 – 1 ¼" x wof strips for single fold binding.

Tan print: Cut 3 – 3 ½" x wof strips for outer border.

Foundation Paper Piecing

See basic paper piecing instructions on page 76.

Assembly

Refer to the quilt photo and lay out the 6 paper pieced blocks and 6 – 4 ½" alternate blocks into 4 rows of 3 blocks each. Stitch a 1 ½" x 4 ½" green print sashing strip between each block. Press the seams toward the sashing. Stitch a 1 ½" x 14 ½" sashing strip between the rows and on the top and bottom. Press the seams toward the sashing.

Prairie Points

Make 32 Prairie Points with open folds at the center:

Fold a 3" square straight across along its midpoint, wrong sides together. Place the folded square in front of you, with its folded side up. Fold the folded edge down at each side to create a triangle with an open fold at its center. Press slightly to keep the folds in place.

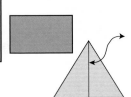

Make a total of 32 prairie points. Arrange them around your quilt, starting at a corner with points and inner border right sides together. The opening of the prairie point should face the inner border. There are 7 prairie points around top and bottom and 9 around the side borders. Adjust them to fit. The triangle tips should point toward the center of the quilt. Baste the prairie points in place, using a ⅛" seam.

Stitch together the 3 – 3 ½" tan print border strips into one strip. Measure your quilt top from top to bottom through the center (21 ½"). Cut 2 - 3 ½" outer borders strips to this length. Stitch one to each side of the quilt. Measure the quilt from side to side through the center (20 ½"). Cut 2 – 3 ½" outer border strips to this length. Stitch one to the top and one to the bottom of the quilt. Press the prairie points toward the outer borders. If desired, stitch each point down with a button.

Finishing

Quilt as desired. Bind with single fold binding.

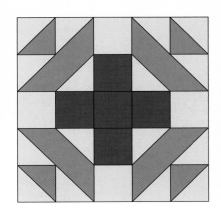

Doll Quilt – Red Cross Block

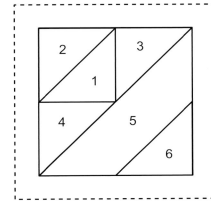

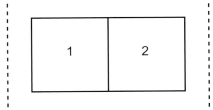

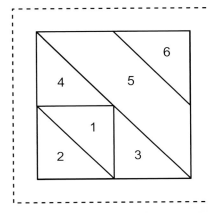

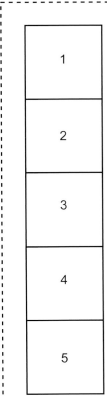

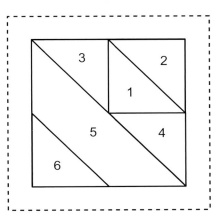

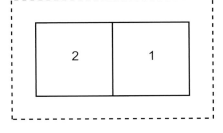

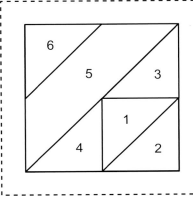

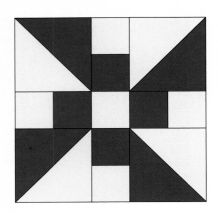

Doll Quilt – Propeller Block

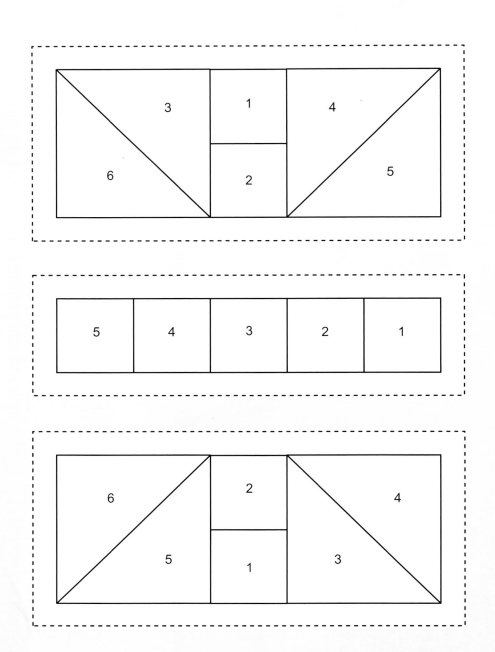

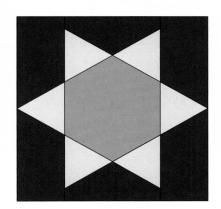

Doll Quilt – Kiowa Star Block

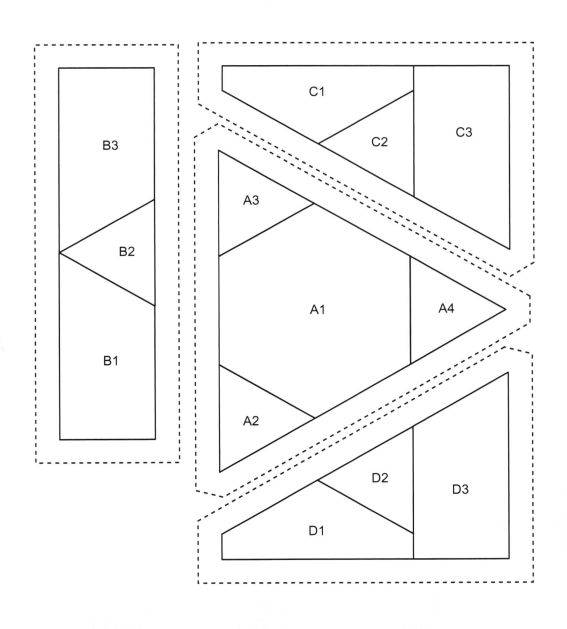

Doll Quilt – Rosebud Block

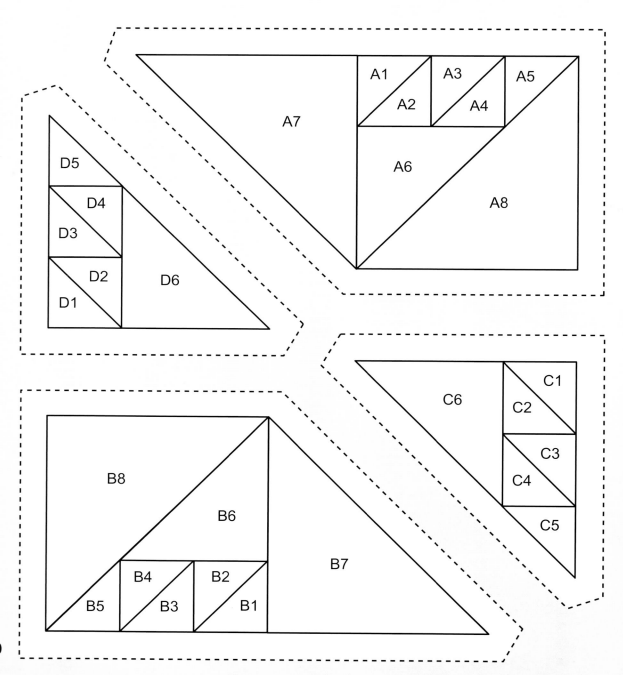

A1 A3 A5
A2 A4
A7
A6
A8

D5
D4
D3
D2
D1 D6

C6 C1
C2
C3
C4
C5

B8
B6
B4 B2
B5 B3 B1
B7

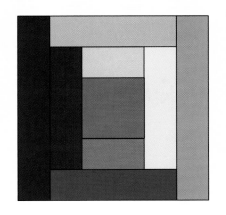

Doll Quilt –
Courthouse Steps Block

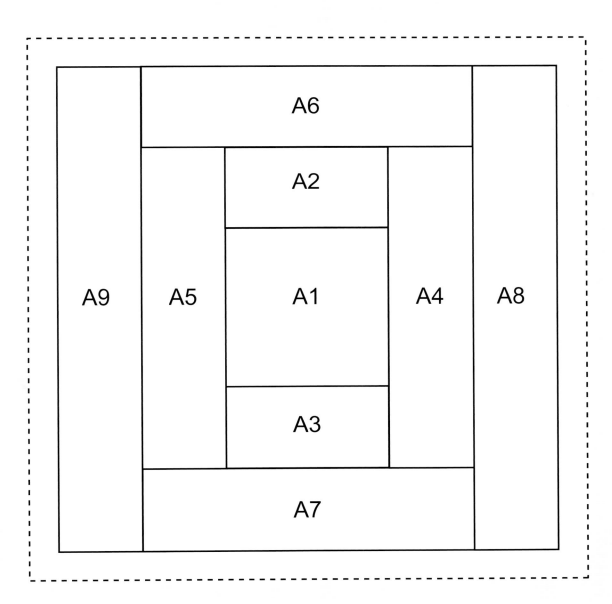

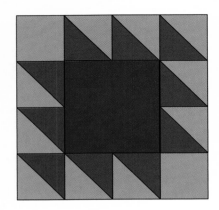

Doll Quilt – Lucy's Star Block

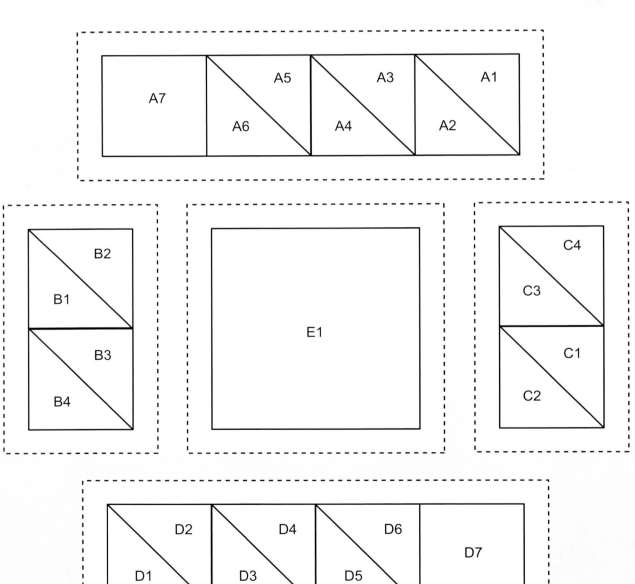

Linda Potter designed and pieced this adorable baby quilt with her grandsons in mind. What little guy wouldn't love to drag this quilt around as he daydreams soaring high above the clouds? Linda has the wonderful ability to piece a whole quilt top while most of us are still just talking about it!

Fabric Requirements

½ yard white for propeller block background

⅜ yard medium blue for propeller block

⅝ yard sky blue for plane background

¼ yard yellow for plane wings

¼ yard green for plane body

⅛ yard red or scraps for plane propeller

¼ yard yellow for inner border

¾ yard green for outer border and binding

Cutting Instructions

White: Cut 6 – 2 ¼" squares (B) for propeller block center.

Cut 24 – 2 ¼" x 2 ⅜" rectangles for (C) for propeller block.

Cut 12 - 4 ½" squares for (A) half-square triangles.

Medium Blue: Cut 24 – 2 ¼" squares (B) for propeller block.
Cut 12 - 4 ½" squares for (A) half-square triangles.

Yellow: Cut 4 - 1 ½" x wof for inner border.

Green: Cut 4 - 3 ½" x wof for outer border.
Cut 4 - 2 ¼" x wof for binding.

Propeller Block

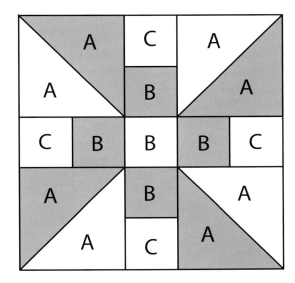

Piecing Instructions

1. Draw a diagonal line on the back of each 4 ½" white square.

2. Place a 4 ½" medium blue square and a 4 ½" white square with right sides together. Sew ¼" on each side of the diagonal line. Cut on the diagonal line. Press the seam toward the medium blue triangle. Make 24 – 4 ¼" unfinished white/medium blue half-square triangles.

3. Stitch together a (B) medium blue 2 ¼" square and (C) white 2 ¼" x 2 ⅜" rectangle. Make 24.

4. Stitch together a B/C unit on each side of a (B) white 2 ¼" square. Make 6.

5. Stitch a white/medium blue half-square triangle on each side of a B/C unit. Note the orientation of the medium blue. Make 12.

6. Refer to the block diagram and stitch the units together into 3 rows. Press the seams away from the triangles. Stitch the rows together. Press the seams toward the middle. The unfinished block measures 9 ½" square. Make 6.

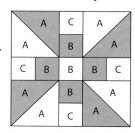

Plane Block

Paper Piecing Instructions

We made this block with basic paper piecing.

Refer to the photo for color placement. Piece each pattern section separately and then sew them all together. It is helpful to use a smaller stitch length and a larger needle (9/14). Cutting does not have to be precise, but the fabric piece needs to be at least ½" larger on all sides of the numbered piece it corresponds to.

There are several types of foundation piecing papers you can buy. We use vellum and have very good luck with it.

Make a photocopy of each section.

First, sew the line between pieces #1 and #2.

Lay the #1 fabric piece (wrong side down) on the back side of the printed foundation paper.

Be sure the fabric covers all of piece #1. Next, place your #2 fabric right sides together extending the raw edge at least ¼" over the seam line between #1 and #2. Sew on the side of the paper with the print on it, going a stitch or two past the intersecting lines. Make sure when you fold it back over #2 it will cover the piece plus ¼" seam allowance for the next seams. Finger press or use a small iron. Trim your seam to ¼".

Continue sewing in this manner until all numbered sections are complete. Leave a ¼" seam allowance, then trim the edges.

Sew the sections together. Press your block, lightly spray starching. Trim your block, paying attention to the outside ¼" seam allowance. Make 6 blocks.

Remove the paper from the back by lightly spritzing it with water. Start at the centers, not the corners. You may need tweezers to remove some of the tiny pieces. Some people like to leave the paper in until they have sewn all the blocks together.

Assemble the center following the quilt photo, alternating the plane and propeller blocks.

Borders and Binding

Measure the quilt from top to bottom in several places. Take an average of these measurements. Cut 2 – 1 ½" yellow strips to this measurement. Sew to each side of the quilt. Measure the quilt from side to side in several places. Take an average of these measurements. Cut 2 – 1 ½" yellow strips to this measurement. Sew to the top and bottom of the quilt.

Repeat the measuring process, and cut the 3 ½" green strips for the sides and stitch. Repeat for the top and bottom borders.

Finishing

Quilt as desired. Our quilter quilted the name of Amelia Earhart's planes: Linnet airstream; Red Bus; Spirit of Mercury; and Flying Mercury in the inner yellow border. Use the 2 ¼" strips sewn together to make the binding. Bind, using your favorite method.

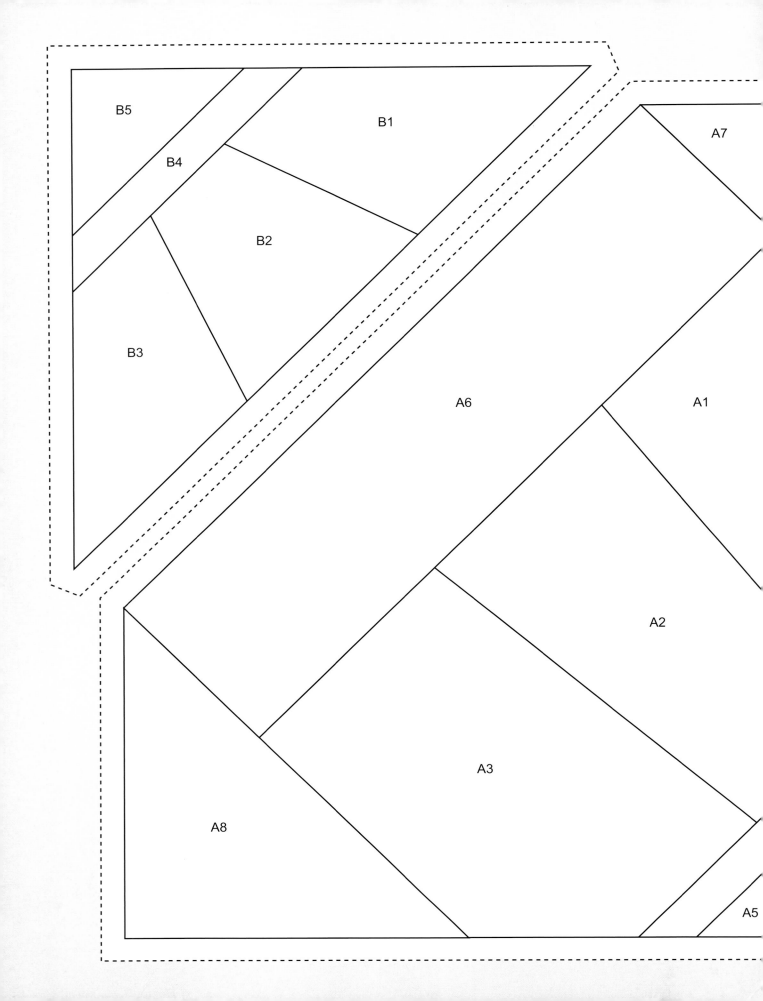

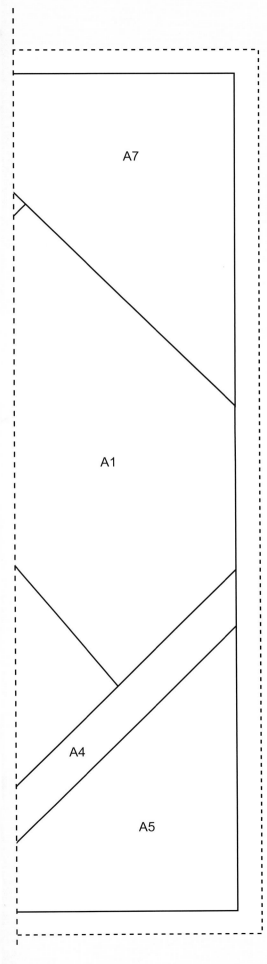

A7

A1

A4

A5